needles of itching feathers

jared schickling

the operating system c. 2018

the operating system print//document chapbook

needles of itching feathers

ISBN: 978-1-946031-38-9
copyright © 2018 by Jared Schickling
edited and designed by Lynne DeSilva-Johnson with poetry editor Peter Milne Greiner

is released under a Creative Commons CC-BY-NC-ND (Attribution, Non Commercial, No Derivatives) License: its reproduction is encouraged for those who otherwise could not afford its purchase in the case of academic, personal, and other creative usage from which no profit will accrue. Complete rules and restrictions are available at: http://creativecommons.org/licenses/by-nc-nd/3.0/
For additional questions regarding reproduction, quotation, or to request a pdf for review contact operator@theoperatingsystem.org

This text was set in The Constellation of Heracles, Minion, Franchise, and OCR-A Standard.
Books from The Operating System are distributed to the trade by SPD/Small Press Distribution, with ePub and POD via Ingram, with production by Spencer Printing, in Honesdale, PA, in the USA.

Cover Art uses a 1943 nitrate negative from Esther Bubley's FSA/Office of War Information holdings, in the public domain. Notes on the negative read: "Washington, D.C. Feeding the pigeons in Lafayette Park. This woman has been bringing grain to the pigeons almost daily for thirteen years,"

The operating system is a member of the Radical Open Access Collective, a community of scholar-led, not-for-profit presses, journals and other open access projects. Now consisting of 40 members, we promote a progressive vision for open publishing in the humanities and social sciences.
Learn more at: http://radicaloa.disruptivemedia.org.uk/about/

Your donation makes our publications, platform and programs possible! We <3 You.
bit.ly/growtheoperatingsystem

the operating system
141 Spencer Street #203
Brooklyn, NY 11205
www.theoperatingsystem.org
operator@theoperatingsystem.org

needles of itching feathers

jared schichling

KIDS

If the apathy of the evening continues
and presently the moon rises and living goes
to the late dailiness that repressed it,
if in the cleared air
the hellish forgetting of the planet
on a sunny day does dim mortally,
if a dark stability of boots in the dirt
conceals the sound in the seeds,
if the day once again chafes like an irritant
and turns into a furnace of land and air
if the weed does pollinate,
if the easy trellis lives,
if the seed and taste of the thorns
appears in the starry puddle,
they will know they are still awake:
they will forget
what they could not keep for themselves,
nights when the joy in their ears
displaced the sound of the genesis.

DISEMBODIED EMOTIONS TO FEEL BUT NOT EXPLAIN

realization of each passerby life as vivid and complex as its own ambiguous intensity of looking someone in the eyes simultaneously invasive and vulnerable subtly aggressive fucking resistant feeling of being out of place bittersweet having arrived the future seeing how it's turning out as never yet incapable of telling its past selves

not wanting to, that is strange comeuppance of used bookshops sweatshops awareness unsettles its own heartbeat that eerie, forlorn atmosphere of a stolen place that is usually bustling with people but is not now abandoned and finally quiet inexplicable urge to push people away especially close friends it really likes hypothetical conversations playing out in its heads like the amniotic tranquility of a thunderstorm indoors

the frustration of photographic something amazing when millions of identical pages already exist, a conversation in which everyone is talking, a sadness that it will never be able to know something for everyone, a state of exhaustion inspired by senselessness endlessnesses desire to be struck by disasters plane crash, survivors, lose everything in a fire having no one to blame would be ideal though no one when someone relates to it

no one would seem to give up talking the tendency to give up talking or trying to, anyway how long it takes to know something or someone, like something returning home from the memorable immersion only to find it faded rapidly in its mind realizing the plot of its life doesn't make sense to it anymore like some conspiracy, in its mind sense of being stuck in just one body only one place at one time incorrigible and careless about it to care

less, weary with the same old issues it's always had being it, of course, the same boring flaws and anxieties that it's been gnawing on for days how many days in the smallness of perspective

VOICE READER

You tell the truth. You are inclined to be careful and practical, causing you to succeed repeatedly. Everyone knows you are smart.

You have a poor imagination. You trail the intelligence community. You have no influence over your associates. People love you for hiding your power. You don't screw small animals.

You possess confidence and are generally brave. You're the renter type. You esteem most people. You are easy going, patient and open to advice. You are gentle.

You are impractical and a quitter. With a dogged determination to be. Slothful. Most of us know you are pliant and malleable. You are nothing but a goddamn capitalist.

You are dull and dimwitted. People like you because you are heterosexual. You thrive on exogamy. However, you are inclined to expect too little for too much. This means you are expensive.

You are immune to and forgetful of other people's problems. They know you're no sucker. You are always starting early and that is why you'll seldom be on welfare and always be worth shit.

You consider yourself a born follower while we know you're a pushover. Certainly you are a protector. You are selfless and can tolerate honest criticism. Your humility is disgusting. You are always doing charity.

You are the illogical type and hate order, a slovenliness sickening to friends. We are warm and emotional and never fall asleep making love as excellent bus riders and whores.

You are the business type and have a difficult time without a social reality. If you are a man you are most likely straight. Chances of employment and monetary gains remain high. Most of your women make excellent pimps. Most survive venereal disease.

You are dumb in art and can be trusted. All shall achieve the pinnacle of failure from the tyranny of your ethics. A plu-perfect son-of-a-bitch you are not. Most of you escape murder.

You are pessimistic and depressed. You have no plan thanks to this surfeit of talent. The majority of you are sober and health nuts. People laugh at you because you are always winning.

You're liberal and afraid of not gambling. You'll do anything and are energetic. There has never been one like you who wasn't important. You should stand still for long periods of time to attract pigeons. You are good at squelching farts in church.

BUTTERFLY VISITS TURTLE'S EYES

attracted to old fruit
whose behavior is opportunistic
to drink decaying fruit
like some carrion are attracted
full of sodium
and ammonium ions, sugars
rotting tissues of fruits
alcohols of the metabolic process
metabolic fuel
of decaying things
certain moist substances
like rotting plant matter
mud and carrion
release the fluid

COUNTERFACTUAL COMMUNICATION AT HOME

*It isn't as bizarre as it sounds. The conditions appear
when a system is repeatedly measured.
Creating a frozen system with a very high probability.*

Has the existence of holographic technology
begged the question? Can a phase of light itself
be used for imaging?
The answer is yes?

The phase of light itself
became the carrier of information?

Run a channel between two sites? This system is frozen
in a certain state? It can always be discarded
and a new one set up?

Light is described by waves
but not by particles? It is the perfect vehicle?

If I embed the image in the light
and the message can be transmitted

without actually sending anything?
The intensity of the light will not matter one bit?
Results must now be verified
by an external source?

THE ARCHITECT

That homicidal bird impales
them on thorns and barbed wire

Aggressive is this dumb bird
begging

That dopey legged raptor's a fraud
with carrion

And this one's the worst
stashing garbage for shame

eating later one morning
I wake up

to all that stupid singing I realize
Canada is not South

THE STRANGE BIRD WITH TWO HEADS WHO HEARD NOTHING

Two heads on a bird
facing right and left. When the left saw
a sweet red fruit
the bird swooped down
to pluck it. It plucked it
and sat beside the river
eating it. The right head said
could you spare some please
but the left, knowing it only needed
one stomach
said nothing. The right head

said nothing. Soon
soaring high again
the right side of the bird
saw a sweet red fruit
so the bird swooped down
to pluck it. But the bird in this tree
hearing it's poison, it will kill you
plucked it
and sat beside the river
eating it. The left head said

please stop, don't eat it.
But the right, knowing it'd
been cheated
and feeling good now
said nothing. And that is how
the bird died.

MORE LIKE A GREAT THOUGHT THAN A GREAT MACHINE

"The atoms of our bodies
are traceable to stars that
produced them in their cores

"And spewed these enriched ingredients
pooping across the galaxy
a long time ago and

"For this reason, we are connected
to the world, connected
to the earth, and connected

"To the universe, dust
for whom things only exist
by designation

IT'S ALL AROUND US (CUT OFF)

The closest living relative to Tyrannosaurus Rex
is a chicken, birds kept as pets
like doves, parakeets, lovebirds
live naturally in pairs. The smallest bird egg
belongs to the hummingbird
it's the size of a pea. The largest
from the ostrich
is a cantaloupe. A bird's eye consumes
fifty percent of a bird's head
the penguin can swim but not fly, it does
walk upright. Owl head swivels in a circle
but cannot move its eyes
chicken makes two hundred distinct
communiqués. When it comes to birds
the male has glamorous feathers, coloration
songs and dances, female chooses its mate
on how attractive it finds it.
Documented homosexual and/or transgender behavior
in five hundred species
as of nineteen ninety nine. An estimated third of all
bird owners leave the radio on
for their pets. Reptiles were laying eggs
long before chickens appeared.
The goose was the first
domesticated bird. Kiwi birds are blind
so they hunt by smell. Several breeds of chicken
lay colored eggs, like green or blue
or brown, the common phrase "eat like a bird"

means "eat like a pig." A gathering of larks
is an exaltation, a group of chickens
is a peep. A smattering of geese
is a gaggle, a swarm of ravens
is a murder. A nightmare of owls
is a parliament. Chickens
laying brown eggs have
red ear lobes. A genetic link is
between the two. Crows have the largest
cerebral hemispheres, mockingbirds can imitate
many sounds.

REFLECTIONS

It takes on the characteristics
of those looking. Kids will for sale
enquire within. It takes on the characteristics
of those looking. Where hunger is a market
in flesh, parents and siblings eat
dead relatives. It takes on the characteristics
of those looking. Two years after her death caught
freezing it. It takes on the characteristics
of those looking. A fully grown adolescent attacks
school with a sword. It takes on the characteristics
of those looking. He pauses for photos and damage is
minimal. It takes on the characteristics
of those looking. An earthly eruption kills twenty
thousand. It takes on the characteristics
of those looking. The face of the only survivor swells
eyes blanch red, hands white, and she begins to
hallucinate. It takes on the characteristics
of those looking. The man in flippers finding
a lifeless body. It takes on the characteristics
of those looking. A father sits and stares at the severed
hands of his daughter eaten
by a rubber company's militia. It takes on the characteristics
of those looking. He fails to meet
the collection quota. It takes on the characteristics
of those looking. The professional photographer we know
his story. It takes on the characteristics
of those looking. He'll proffer fifty bucks and leave

his photos. It takes on the characteristics
of those looking. I don't think I would make
a good wife for anybody, will say the note. It takes on the characteristics
of those looking. They find her in the catacombs
by an honest mistake, but no one can confirm
who the body is. It takes on the characteristics
of those looking.

FROZEN FOOD LIGHT

Pollutant in its blubber like a hole in the pocket!
Killed the unborn calf and left the pod barren, but happiness!
Like insurance from its job!
Was a still state of mind, I needed what I wanted!
Said even the whale, perhaps surviving!
In no short time, every substance moving!
Strangely, round the food web, it must have tasted so much loving!
it so, For their lives, accumulating, altering, adapting but hit!
Glass ceilings, whole stockpiles!
In a hole, its pocket, evolving!
Ways to escape this, evolved!
Ways to pollute this, spending so much time together!
Like a natural stalemate, burying the dead!
But for getting for years!
When the deep freeze melted!
On languid banks, a hoary spring!
In the permafrost, love exposed!
Fell into the water!

SOME THING

In the woods that night
the car horn returns and faded;
I talk the whole time, until the day:
like an experience it gladdens me.

The future is now passing by that talking

Involuntarily it's included
in the squared chore where I as I
still in my presence:
by that street a feathered skin
expands among the columns of bushes.

FREQUENT DREAMS OF CROWS

I forget you on fine nights!
You would close the door like the stump
to whisper the dream. You abhor
the malignant disappearance of bugs

and worms. The sea contracted
blue limitations. It was the organized
inefficient drying, the porous
agitation. It was the unpromising night:

with scientific plastic pins
you unbraided and freed my butterfly.
Broken cycles of a warm room

you took from such bland bark,
day clothes and winter hat,
needle of itching feathers.

MOB

My foot on the nail in summer lost
to winter's coming
heat. Hard skulls could relinquish
shoes there, when days

followed me lighted outside
to a pond without trees that hated
my fancy duds.
In the birds' short-lived silence,

around each nowhere city,
I forgot my dangling foot…
cabin of thorns we

missed health, kept trinkets. Exhausted and
aged, we burned bridges, feet,
we stopped the public in the swamp.

POETS WHO DON'T DRIVE

"It's not just that it's
leaning but
it's really

trained to move

"With tremendous feeling
on the least hints
and how to manage

an enormous keel

CHORES REDUX

It's a sunny day in
a small town, you make your way
the road and houses
gave way, this is where

you dump the ashes
and drive away.

NEGATIVE

A scar followed the relaxed
image in the window.

Among the many like
trees. Like used

socks. In a pile.
Home. Dull day

of leaked presence.
The image in the window.

WHEN I WAS YOUR AGE

nights when the wind talked a little
and the feet split in
abstraction

When the clack of alert pipes
finally settles in the yard, broken
glass, time flew

When yr cold, when yr zoological inertia
with demonic and/or saintly resignation
steals simple and impatient

Lives, substantial
simulations, yr straight lines
of surfacing roots

Grateful acknowledgment is made
to the editors at *Unlikely Stories Mark V*
for first publishing some of these.

JARED SCHICKLING's most recent books of poetry are *Needles of Itching Feathers* and *The Mercury Poem* (BlazeVOX, 2017). Other books include *Province of Numb Errs* (2016), *The Paranoid Reader: Essays, 2006-2012* (Furniture Press, 2014), *Prospectus for a Stage* (LRL Textile Series, 2014), and he edited *A Lyrebird: Selected Poems of Michael Farrell* (BlazeVOX, 2017). He lives in Western New York and edits Delete Press and The Mute Canary, publishers of poetry.

WHY PRINT DOCUMENT?

The Operating System uses the language "print document" to differentiate from the book-object as part of our mission to distinguish the act of documentation-in-book-FORM from the act of publishing as a backwards-facing replication of the book's agentive *role* as it may have appeared the last several centuries of its history. Ultimately, I approach the book as TECHNOLOGY: one of a variety of printed documents (in this case, bound*) that humans have invented and in turn used to archive and disseminate ideas, beliefs, stories, and other evidence of production.*

Ownership and use of printing presses and access to (or restriction of printed materials) has long been a site of struggle, related in many ways to revolutionary activity and the fight for civil rights and free speech all over the world. While (in many countries) the contemporary quotidian landscape has indeed drastically shifted in its access to platforms for sharing information and in the widespread ability to "publish" digitally, even with extremely limited resources, the importance of publication on physical media has not diminished. In fact, this may be the most critical time in recent history for activist groups, artists, and others to insist upon learning, establishing, and encouraging personal and community documentation practices. Hear me out.

With The OS's print endeavors I wanted to open up a conversation about this: the ultimately radical, transgressive act of creating PRINT /DOCUMENTATION in the digital age. It's a question of the archive, and of history: who gets to tell the story, and what evidence of our life, our behaviors, our experiences are we leaving behind? We can know little to nothing about the future into which we're leaving an unprecedentedly digital document trail — but we can be assured that publications, government agencies, museums, schools, and other institutional powers that be will continue to leave BOTH a digital and print version of their production for the official record. Will we?

As a (rogue) anthropologist and long time academic, I can easily pull up many accounts about how lives, behaviors, experiences — how THE STORY of a time or place — was pieced together using the deep study of correspondence, notebooks, and other physical documents which are no longer the norm in many lives and practices. As we move our creative behaviors towards digital note taking, and even audio and video, what can we predict about future technology that is in any way assuring that our stories will be accurately told – or told at all? How will we leave these things for the record?

In these documents we say: WE WERE HERE, WE EXISTED, WE HAVE A DIFFERENT STORY

- Lynne DeSilva-Johnson, Founder/Managing Editor,
   THE OPERATING SYSTEM, Brooklyn NY 2017

*poetics and process: a conversation
with jared schickling and lynne desilva-johnson*

Greetings comrade! Thank you for talking to us about your process today!

Likewise, greetings.   It is my pleasure.

Can you introduce yourself, in a way that you would choose?

I don't know that I can!   Who "am" I—what is this "I"—this person was born, 1978, raised in the 80s, not exactly by choice, certainly without another option; at some point along the way, "I" must have spontaneously appeared and am currently residing along the Niagara Escarpment, north of Buffalo, on the eastern fringes of a National Sacrifice Zone.   At locks 34 and 35 along the Erie Canal, Lockport has its own resident Superfund site.   A wise person might try—which I did, or thought I was—to escape the place, not embrace it but, nonetheless, I feel attached to here.   Mollie, my wife, is from the orchards down the road, Medina. It's in our blood, I guess.   We returned after some years of traveling and working to raise our family, which grew and shrank with the introduction of kids and the deaths of a cat and the dogs.   The other cat—the O.G. of them all who brought Mollie and I together—is still hanging around.   She reminds me of Bartleby, except that she is loved.   Our situation seems precarious and filled with adventure, as Mollie manages a seasonal bakery on a farm and I cobble together teaching gigs and otherwise.   Some years ago I acquired some kayaks, and between February and June can be found floating in the flooded solitude of the neighboring swamps.

Why are you a poet/writer/artist?

I don't think I know.   Should something like that—for myself, at least—be explained?   Does it need explaining—It?   I would not call it a choice, exactly.

Not doing it is impossible. I've tried it. I can't help it, frankly.

I enjoy the language that goes where language cannot, and just so am a consumer of all genres and most disciplines. Aspects of the text or otherwise at hand plus my reasons for being there equal how much time I commit to it, and in the end write far more poetry than anything else because, for whatever reason, it is the form in which I am most comfortable fleshing out ideas on the page. The associative nature of it seems amenable to connecting the dots, given my consumption habits. I like the idea of using ever fewer words to express a complexity, and yet I find myself reveling for now in Melville's Pierre.

Thoreau is right, though, that writing is the art form closest to the human being, as texts must be carved out of the breath of life itself. Only through reading can the dead resurrect themselves. Music is close to the text in its bodily dimensions, but listening is less active than reading (which involves listening). And whereas music tends to muzzle noise by introducing a select aural experience into the environment, literature, through visual and aural means, tends to amplify noise in its natural, organic dimensions.

When did you decide you were a poet/writer/artist (and/or: do you feel comfortable calling yourself a poet/writer/artist, what other titles or affiliations do you prefer/feel are more accurate)?

I am a poet, though I don't put much thought or stock into the fact. Living in the world prevents me from doing so. The alarm will go off. There is something active and vibrant in refusing to "value" my life as a poet. It keeps me focused on poetry itself, perhaps. I suppose it's also simply my own way of relating to what it is I do.

As to when I started as a poet, it's a story I hesitate to tell because I know it too well. It sounds redundant. Around 1997 or 98 I discovered Bob Dylan's Highway 61 Revisited *and memorized "Desolation Row." Two things happened from that. It mentions T. S. Eliot and Ezra Pound "fighting in the captain's tower," so I read*

Eliot. Then, at work, utterly slacking as far as they were concerned, I turned off my gear and wrote out the lyrics, filling in the gaps I couldn't remember with stuff I'd never remember. When I got to the end, I then wrote a poem. And that was that. Two decades later I have fleeting thoughts in earlier memories suggesting "poet," but who really can know. The thing is, I wasn't raised with books, I had to find them; meanwhile, my grandmother had piles of those soft-porn romance novels, from which I'd build forts and castles for imaginary characters, and my adolescence was spent outdoors.

What's a "poet" (or "writer" or "artist") anyway?

Much like love or beauty—you often won't know it when confronted with it.

What do you see as your cultural and social role (in the literary / artistic / creative community and beyond)?

I don't really know. Clearly I have a role, as everyone has a role. Many roles to play. Roles within roles. In addition to writing I work with my friends on Delete Press, and have otherwise done such work, which I've always done without question. Recently I launched another venture, The Mute Canary. The arts have a long history of attending to and informing the cultural and social upheavals of the day. The CIA certainly saw value in propagating American arts overseas during the Cold War, regardless of the art form's actual intent. More recently it looks like the tactics of the #MeToo movement, a profound moment in American history, were proven first among the poets and the "callout culture" they invented on social media. What the Mongrel Coalition accomplished from the perspective of poetics should not be underestimated nor casually brushed aside. And my only point is that American society and the arts are indeed hopelessly entangled; the fact that poetry has and has had an impact beyond the world of poets and their publishing will be obvious enough to anyone who looks at it. As a poet, and a publisher, my own concerns lie chiefly with ecology, relationships.

That said, I think it is always premature for the artist, including the poet, to imagine they understand what their work amounts to. And yet, I understand that having a reason for keeping the light on is necessary, too. Steve McCaffery once told me that—at some point a poet has to ask why they are writing. I hope that answers your question.

Talk about the process or instinct to move these poems (or your work in general) as independent entities into a body of work. How and why did this happen? Have you had this intention for a while? What encouraged and/or confounded this (or a book, in general) coming together? Was it a struggle?

Establishing the sequence of the book was not a struggle. It was extracted from a larger, unpublished project, "Missing (   )," which took shape over a year. That manuscript happened as a singular project, meaning I was not, for the most part, writing singular poems at the time. I was writing a long poem, a book-length poem, partly as a way of forcing myself to stay engaged with my own writing. To arrive at the chapbook I identified certain strains in that work, picked one, and excised what did not belong to it.

Once the basic structure was there, once the pieces appeared there, alone, exposed, some re-vision needed doing—the fun, frustrating part—which of course then finds its way back into the original whole—re-writing from the inside out—this circuit or, more properly, feedback loop (given the magnitude of perturbation at each turn) might have repeated a few times.

Did you envision this collection as a collection or understand your process as writing or making specifically around a theme while the poems themselves were being written / the work was being made? How or how not?

Your questions give me pause. Even though I was consciously writing a book-length poem, I wouldn't say I was conscious of the book I was writing. A deliberate effort, to be sure, but through accretion, where poem is worked on and worked over many times before and after others join it, onward, in loops. I describe the whole because, like a bird that laid an egg, it's what let the smaller chapbook happen, which then passed through a similar gauntlet.

The chapbook, I would say, finds pleasure's pulse in the precarious state of the psychological fascia still keeping us human. As the tissue stretches and tears, birds fly in.

What formal structures or other constrictive practices (if any) do you use in the creation of your work? Have certain teachers or instructive environments, or readings/writings/work of other creative people informed the way you work/write?

Because I read poems of the sort, I will often dabble in so-called "inherited" forms which, to greater or lesser degrees, prove only to be starting places. The methods I use are my own, or have been internalized so deeply through practice that I no longer recognize them, and I am indiscriminate of form—any and all modes should apply. In thinking about the possibilities for criticism and the handling of historical material, or news, both through and beyond poetry, Barthes (S/Z and The Pleasure of the Text), Federman, and Reznikoff have been instructive. Theresa Hak Kyung Cha's Dictée seeped into my work in ways I haven't tried to account for yet. In terms of philosophy, I look to Dickinson and Melville for sustenance more frequently with time. I hesitate to go too closely to these places, though, because my true interests range widely.

I also enjoy abecedarians. All kinds, especially for kids, Edward Lear or Edward Gorey or the elaborately intoxicating Chicka Chicka Boom Boom. I don't know why. I've written two.

Speaking of monikers, what does your title represent? How was it generated? Talk about the way you titled the book, and how your process of naming (individual pieces, sections, etc) influences you and/or colors your work specifically.

Well, there are a lot of birds in the chapbook, ornithology in various ways, so I thought it was important to capture that. But there's a lot of death and boredom and violence undergirding all the life and exuberance and beauty, as the book is adjacent to something amoral. There is also a personal, quasi-autobiographical whiff about it, something I hadn't realized until afterward. It caught me off guard and, through many re-readings and the like, I couldn't shake the feeling. I don't think I write from a self-involved perspective and tend to get rid of it later when I do. In this case I let it stay and let the birds in and amplified it, which was utterly disconcerting, especially given those birds. It is perhaps a subtlety that won't be noticed, but I see it. So, all in all, "needles of itching feathers."

What does this particular work represent to you as indicative of your method/creative practice? your history? your mission/intentions/hopes/plans?

It is indicative of a time and place. In my work, not just here but in all of it, the places are real, and most of it depicts events as they happened. I use the term "event" loosely to make room for the imagination—the contested, prime real estate of "place."

What does this book DO (as much as what it says or contains)?

It does nothing. Actively. Which is something, I suppose.

The reader, however, will do more. If this book can be a part of that, then it will have served a purpose.

What would be the best possible outcome for this book? What might it do in the world, and how will its presence as an object facilitate your creative role in your community and beyond? What are your hopes for this book, and for your practice?

My honest answer is that I actively do not think in these terms. I mean, it'd be great if it could do this or that, but this line of inquiry into my own creative intimacies only causes unnecessary problems for my writing. My philosophy is to write and work without attachment to result. I am only increasingly interested in expressing ideas through poems. Non-attachment helps me set aside or, in some cases, slough off entirely itchy intentions and respond to the writing as it happens. It makes me more attentive to what the language is doing.

Let's talk a little bit about the role of poetics and creative community in social activism, in particular in what I call "Civil Rights 2.0," which has remained immediately present all around us in the time leading up to this series' publication. I'd be curious to hear some thoughts on the challenges we face in speaking and publishing across lines of race, age, privilege, social/cultural background, and sexuality within the community, vs. the dangers of remaining and producing in isolated "silos."

When it comes to practicing poetry, I must confess my hermetic preference. I need as much peace and quiet and solitude as possible to effectively practice, to read, think, write, edit, publish, nap, all of it. Indeed I've felt at times that poetry has ruined my life. If so, so be it.

I have also felt at times that literature, particularly transgressive literature, is an inherently childish and therefore evil activity for an adult to somehow enjoy, let alone build their life around, especially where poverty is involved. I am not alone in that sentiment.

However, it is also true that art is the fuel of grassroots activism. It's the vitamins, the very sun and rain. Art opens the mind to what is possible by educating the consumer on what is (or was or will be) in a way that other information venues cannot. It tunes us into a better, more enlightened place than the one we must otherwise endure. Art, however, is not good at governance or policy, which is why it manages to accomplish what it does in the first place: bring diverse groups of people together with shared visions.

Artists do what activists strive to do: find a voice or language to tell a story or paint a picture that, when it is honest, and informed and beautiful, can be shared and/or embraced by others. Activism is a long game whereas art is momentary and yet, oddly enough, progressive politics seems to thrive on art and wither in its absence. Naturally, I'd say, the push for diversity in publishing, as in any other industry, matters and will continue.

As for the challenge of speaking across lines of identity, which I take to mean the difficulty of writing beyond the limits of one's own cultural experience, it amplifies the voices and experiences that history omitted. It is a good challenge—a difficult passage to a better place. I do wonder if we'll ever get to a point on this shrinking planet, since we actually are all in it together now, where identifying labels beyond "human" or, better yet, "animal" won't matter, as it's naïve to think we're anywhere close.

As fast, cheap means of production help publishers flood the market with all kinds of ephemeral poems, ephemeral poets and ephemeral venues, modern technology does present a unique opportunity in the push for diversity. Given that the primary currency among writers is still text (I hope it is, anyway), it is (still) possible to participate in these developments virtually, such that geography and distance from the usual centers of activity become less important. Literally anyone anywhere can and do have their voice(s) heard now.

Is there anything else we should have asked, or that you want to share?

Just a sincere thank-you for what you do.

SELECTED RECENT AND FORTHCOMING OS PRINT/DOCUMENTS

Ark Hive-Marthe Reed [2019]
A Bony Framework for the Tangible Universe-D. Allen [kin(d)*, 2019]
Śnienie / Dreaming - Marta Zelwan/Krystyna Sakowicz,
(Polish-English/dual-language) trans. Victoria Miluch [glossarium, 2019]
Opera on TV-James Brunton [kin(d)*, 2019]
Alparegho: Pareil-À-Rien / Alparegho, Like Nothing Else - Hélène Sanguinetti
(French-English/dual-language), trans. Ann Cefola [glossarium, 2019]
Hall of Waters-Berry Grass [kin(d)*, 2019]
High Tide Of The Eyes - Bijan Elahi (Farsi-English/dual-language)
trans. Rebecca Ruth Gould and Kayvan Tahmasebian [glossarium, 2019]
I Made for You a New Machine and All it Does is Hope - Richard Lucyshyn [2019]
Illusory Borders-Heidi Reszies [2019]
Transitional Object-Adrian Silbernagel [kin(d)*, 2019]
A Year of Misreading the Wildcats [2019]

An Absence So Great and Spontaneous It Is Evidence of Light - Anne Gorrick [2018]
The Book of Everyday Instruction - Chloe Bass [2018]
Executive Orders Vol. II - a collaboration with the Organism for Poetic Research [2018]
One More Revolution - Andrea Mazzariello [2018]
The Suitcase Tree - Filip Marinovich [2018]
Chlorosis - Michael Flatt and Derrick Mund [2018]
Sussuros a Mi Padre - Erick Sáenz [2018]
Sharing Plastic - Blake Nemec [2018]
The Book of Sounds - Mehdi Navid (Farsi dual language, trans. Tina Rahimi) [2018]
In Corpore Sano : Creative Practice and the Challenged Body [Anthology, 2018];
Lynne DeSilva-Johnson and Jay Besemer, co-editors
Abandoners - Lesley Ann Wheeler [2018]
Jazzercise is a Language - Gabriel Ojeda-Sague [2018]
Return Trip / Viaje Al Regreso - Israel Dominguez;
(Spanish-English dual language) trans. Margaret Randall [2018]
Born Again - Ivy Johnson [2018]
Attendance - Rocío Carlos and Rachel McLeod Kaminer [2018]
Singing for Nothing - Wally Swist [2018]
The Ways of the Monster - Jay Besemer [2018]
Walking Away From Explosions in Slow Motion - Gregory Crosby [2018]
The Unspoken - Bob Holman [Bowery Books imprint - 2018]
Field Guide to Autobiography - Melissa Eleftherion [2018]
Kawsay: The Flame of the Jungle - María Vázquez Valdez
(Spanish-English dual language) trans. Margaret Randall [2018]

OS PRINT DOCUMENT ANNUAL CHAPBOOK SERIES TITLES

CHAPBOOK SERIES 2018 : TALES
Greater Grave - Jacq Greyja; Needles of Itching Feathers - Jared Schlickling;
Want-Catcher - Adra Raine; We, The Monstrous - Mark DuCharme

CHAPBOOK SERIES 2017 : INCANTATIONS
featuring original cover art by Barbara Byers
sp. - Susan Charkes; Radio Poems - Jeffrey Cyphers Wright;
Fixing a Witch/Hexing the Stitch - Jacklyn Janeksela;
cosmos a personal voyage by carl sagan ann druyan steven sotor and me - Connie Mae Oliver

CHAPBOOK SERIES 2016: OF SOUND MIND
featuring the quilt drawings of Daphne Taylor
Improper Maps - Alex Crowley; While Listening - Alaina Ferris;
Chords - Peter Longofono; Any Seam or Needlework - Stanford Cheung

CHAPBOOK SERIES 2015: OF SYSTEMS OF
featuring original cover art by Emma Steinkraus
Cyclorama - Davy Knittle; The Sensitive Boy Slumber Party Manifesto - Joseph
Cuillier; Neptune Court - Anton Yakovlev; Schema - Anurak Saelow

CHAPBOOK SERIES 2014: BY HAND
Pull, A Ballad - Maryam Parhizkar;
Can You See that Sound - Jeff Musillo
Executive Producer Chris Carter - Peter Milne Greiner;
Spooky Action at a Distance - Gregory Crosby;

CHAPBOOK SERIES 2013: WOODBLOCK
featuring original prints from Kevin William Reed
Strange Coherence - Bill Considine; The Sword of Things - Tony Hoffman;
Talk About Man Proof - Lancelot Runge / John Kropa;
An Admission as a Warning Against the Value of Our Conclusions - Alexis Quinlan

DOC U MENT
/däkyəmənt/

First meant "instruction" or "evidence," whether written or not.

noun - a piece of written, printed, or electronic matter that provides information or evidence or that serves as an official record
verb - record (something) in written, photographic, or other form
synonyms - paper - deed - record - writing - act - instrument

[Middle English, precept, from Old French, from Latin documentum, example, proof, from docre, to teach; see dek- in Indo-European roots.]

Who is responsible for the manufacture of value?

Based on what supercilious ontology have we landed in a space where we vie against other creative people in vain pursuit of the fleeting credibilities of the scarcity economy, rather than freely collaborating and sharing openly with each other in ecstatic celebration of MAKING?

While we understand and acknowledge the economic pressures and fear-mongering that threatens to dominate and crush the creative impulse, we also believe that ***now more than ever we have the tools to relinquish agency via cooperative means,*** fueled by the fires of the Open Source Movement.

Looking out across the invisible vistas of that rhizomatic parallel country we can begin to see our community beyond constraints, in the place where intention meets resilient, proactive, collaborative organization.

Here is a document born of that belief, sown purely of imagination and will.
When we document we assert. We print to make real, to reify our being there.
When we do so with mindful intention to address our process, to open our work to others, to create beauty in words in space, to respect and acknowledge the strength of the page we now hold physical, a thing in our hand... we remind ourselves that, like Dorothy: *we had the power all along, my dears.*

THE PRINT! DOCUMENT SERIES
is a project of
the trouble with bartleby
in collaboration with
the operating system

www.ingramcontent.com/pod-product-compliance
Lightning Source LLC
Chambersburg PA
CBHW081340080526
44588CB00017B/2691